HOLDING SPACE SERIES
STANDING IN PRAYER FOR YOUR ORDAINED BUSINESS
E. Claudette Freeman, Convener and Editor

©November 2021 by Zora James Publishing
An Imprint of Pecan Tree Publishing
Hollywood, FL 33020
www.zorajamespublishing.com
www.pecantreebooks.com

I0152775

Scripture quotations are from those listed here.

THE AUTHORIZED (KING JAMES) VERSION. Rights in the Authorized Version in the United Kingdom are vested in the Crown. Reproduced by permission of the Crown's patentee, Cambridge University Press.

THE AMPLIFIED BIBLE, Old Testament copyright © 1965, 1987 by the Zondervan Corporation. The Amplified New Testament copyright © 1958, 1987 by The Lockman Foundation. Used by permission.

THE HOLY BIBLE, NEW INTERNATIONAL VERSION ®. Copyright © 1973, 1978, 1984 by International Bible Society. Used by permission of Zondervan Publishing House. All rights reserved.

THE HOLY BIBLE, NEW LIVING TRANSLATION, copyright © 1996, 2004, 2007 by Tyndale House Foundation. Used by permission of Tyndale House Publishers, Inc., Carol Stream, Illinois 60188. All rights reserved.

978-1-7372621-7-6 Paperback
978-1-7372621-8-3 E-Book
Library of Congress Control Number: 2021950155

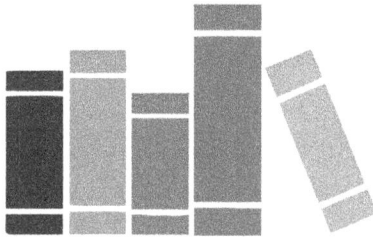

Zora James Publishing

Creating culturally and spiritually necessary
anthologies and collections.

A Pecan Tree Publishing Imprint
www.zorajamespublishing.com
Hollywood, FL

CONTENTS

STANDING IN
PRAYER
FOR YOUR
ORDAINED
BUSINESS

Arranged by

E. CLAUDETTE FREEMAN

INTRODUCTION

HOLDING SPACE SERIES: STANDING IN PRAYER FOR YOUR ORDAINED BUSINESS is book two in the series born to provide encouragement and edification for those in specific industries or categories. Book two focuses on those who are business owners and aspiring entrepreneurs.

The devotionals, prayers and inspiring messages are designed to be your support team on the pathway God has chosen for you. May the words shared here be fuel for your journey, and a match to relight your fire on those challenging days.

The words are holding space - interceding - for you; reminding you that you are not alone, you can fulfill your purpose, you are well able to succeed in your assignment and you were called into The Kingdom for this specific mandate.

At the back of the book is space for you to write out your vision, mission, and a prayer for this season in your own words. There is also a challenge to begin setting aside specific time to consult with God about your entrepreneurial endeavors.

May God be with you, watch over you and provide His prevailing wisdom, strategies, and witty ideas for you.

E. Claudette Freeman, Convener and Editor

OUR SCRIPTURAL MANDATE

I Kings 3:1-9

"And Solomon made affinity with Pharaoh king of Egypt, and took Pharaoh's daughter, and brought her into the city of David, until he had made an end of building his own house, and the house of the LORD, and the wall of Jerusalem round about. Only the people sacrificed in high places because there was no house built unto the name of the LORD, until those days. And Solomon loved the LORD, walking in the statutes of David his father: only he sacrificed and burnt incense in high places. And the king went to Gibeon to sacrifice there; for that was the great high place: a thousand burnt offerings did Solomon offer upon that altar. In Gibeon, the LORD appeared to Solomon in a dream by night: and God said, ask what I shall give thee. And Solomon said, thou hast shewed unto thy servant David my father great mercy, according as he walked before thee in truth, and in righteousness, and in uprightness of heart with thee; and thou hast kept for him this great kindness, that thou hast given him a son to sit on his throne, as it is this day. And now, O LORD my God, thou hast made thy servant king instead of David my father: and I am but a little child: I know not how to go out or come in. And thy servant is in the midst of thy people which thou hast chosen, a great people, that cannot be numbered nor counted for multitude. Give therefore thy servant an understanding heart to judge thy people, that I may discern between good and bad: for who is able to judge this thy so great a people?"

I Kings 8:55-61

*"And he stood and blessed all the congregation of Israel with a loud voice, saying, Blessed be the L*ord*, that hath given rest unto his people Israel, according to all that he promised: there hath not failed one word of all his good promise, which he promised by the hand of Moses his servant. The L*ord *our God be with us, as he was with our fathers: let him not leave us, nor forsake us: That he may incline our hearts unto him, to walk in all his ways, and to keep his commandments, and his statutes, and his judgments, which he commanded our fathers. And let these my words, wherewith I have made supplication before the L*ord*, be nigh unto the L*ord *our God day and night, that he maintain the cause of his servant, and the cause of his people Israel at all times, as the matter shall require. That all the people of the Earth may know that the L*ord *is God, and that there is none else. Let your heart therefore be perfect with the L*ord *our God, to walk in his statutes, and to keep his commandments, as at this day."*

I Kings 5:13-18

"And King Solomon raised a levy out of all Israel; and the levy was thirty thousand men. And he sent them to Lebanon, ten thousand a month by courses: a month they were in Lebanon, and two months at home: and Adoniram was over the levy. And Solomon had threescore and ten thousand that bare burdens, and fourscore thousand hewers in the mountains; Beside the chief of Solomon's officers which were over the work, three thousand and three hundred, which ruled over the people that wrought in the work. And the king commanded, and they brought great stones, costly stones, and hewed stones, to lay the foundation of the house. And Solomon's builders and Hiram's builders did hew them, and the stonesquarers: so, they prepared timber and stones to build the house."

I Kings 7: 13, 14

"And King Solomon sent and fetched Hiram out of Tyre. He was a widow's son of the tribe of Naphtali, and his father was a man of Tyre, a worker in brass: and he was filled with wisdom, and understanding, and cunning to work all works in brass. And he came to King Solomon and wrought all his work."

I Kings 9:26-28

"And King Solomon made a navy of ships in Eziongeber, which is beside Eloth, on the shore of the Red Sea, in the land of Edom. And Hiram sent in the navy his servants, shipmen that had knowledge of the sea, with the servants of Solomon. And they came to Ophir, and fetched from thence gold, four hundred and twenty talents, and brought it to King Solomon."

I Kings 10:15, 28

(15) "Beside that he had of the merchantmen, and of the traffick of the spice merchants, and of all the kings of Arabia, and of the governors of the country."

(28) "And Solomon had horses brought out of Egypt, and linen yarn: the king's merchants received the linen yarn at a price."

OPENING DECLARATION

Released to Release the Gift

Min. Teraleen Campbell

Truthfully speaking, being an entrepreneur is not for the faint of heart. Truth is that the journey involves a rollercoaster ride a great deal of the way. There are days when business is plentiful and others when it is scarce. We awake on some mornings full of enthusiasm, feeling as though we will be super successful, but on others we wonder why we got into this. We second guess our decisions and cause ourselves stress.

This may sound elementary, but I submit this to you, the key is to remind yourself of your WHY. Why did I become an entrepreneur in the first place? Then answer your own question.

- To increase income - the saying goes, if you do what you love then you'll never work another day in your life
- To gain independence – financial and work-life balance
- Financial stability – build wealth for future generations
- Satisfy a need – you are the response to someone's need. You're the answer to a prayer, filler of a void
- Purpose – God has called you to this

Your why will get you through the most difficult days.

I have battled with the tendency to self-sabotage my efforts due to fear and doubt. I know that I am not alone in doubting whether I have what it takes; nor in doubting the gifts and talents that God has placed in me. Consequently, I have, periodically, put those gifts on discount, at rates below what was profitable.

Entrepreneurship also involves humbling yourself. It involves acknowledging that there are things that you don't know and seeking help to acquire that knowledge for the enhancement of your business. You may fulfill those needs by way of achieving a degree, obtaining certification, completing an online seminar, or hiring a consultant.

This journey also involves developing the ability to get over yourself. I cannot tell you the number of times that I have gone to battle with my inner me. I've fought through doubt, fear, lack of focus, isolation and even stubbornness. Alas, the Lord gently reminds me that He has placed gifts inside of me. Those gifts were purposed to serve a designated population and a specific purpose for that population. Therefore, it is not for me to hold onto those gifts; no, they must be released.

The overall blessing is not monetary or material. The blessing is that God indeed does give us grace to release that which He has planted inside so that we can run this entrepreneurial race. We've got this because He has us!

PRAYER

Lord, I pray for you for every businessowner and entrepreneur who is blessed with these words and the gifts and talents that you have bestowed upon them. May they never be taken for granted. I thank you for blessing the works of their hands. I thank you that their business is the solution to someone's problem. Yes, they are answered prayer!

Father, in Jesus' name, I thank you for freeing them to apply their skills and intellect to their business endeavors. I bless You for blessing them with the ability to lead their business, be it a profit or nonprofit entity. I ask that their skills be used to Your glory.

I pray, Kind Father, that You send those who believe in the business that You have given them. Help them to see the vision. I pray that You send people who will not only see it, but who are willing to invest, either with their time or by becoming patrons who will purchase what they have to offer them. Send influencers and help them to establish divine connections Lord, in Jesus' name.

I pray that You give them strategies for the endeavors before them. Give them strategies for future growth, strategies for marketing and strategies that will help make sure the finances of their business are managed properly.

Allow their thoughts to flow creatively and to bring forth creative strategies that will further their business opportunities.

I come against the tactics of the devil that will try to frustrate them and make them doubt themselves. I bind the spirits of jealously, competition, and malice. I also come against feelings of inadequacy and loneliness. I ask Lord that You provide assurance even during those times when they feel isolated and alone.

God empower Your people to overcome every struggle. Increase discernment so they know who to share their goals and strategies with. Help them to know who they can trust.

For the one who is teetering on the edge, I ask that You restore to them the joy in serving their customers. Help them not to allow service to be a yoke but let it be liberating.

In the name of Jesus, I declare these words to be so. Amen!

AFFIRMATIONS

I decree and declare that God has graced me to be the answer to someone's prayer.

I am the solution to a situation.

I am the head and not the tail. I am above and not beneath.

I am the vessel of the Lord who will help those members of my local and the global community.

DEVOTIONAL

ACTIVATING YOUR GIFTS IN THE MARKETPLACE

Min. Sarita Price

"A man's gift makes room for him and brings him before great men." (Proverbs 18:16, NKJV)

It was always mind boggling to me that others could not see the connection between marketplace concepts and biblical principles. How could they not see how they are so easily connected? As a business major with a degree in human resources, I could always relate to the teachings in the Bible and how to apply them to the workplace. For many years I worked in finance before I began my human resources career. I also worked in finance and project management. How could no one see how the stories and guideposts in the Bible on finance, processes, and improvement. It was right there in the Word of God.

After taking a spiritual gift analysis, I scored extremely high in the areas of administration, exhortation, and prophecy. It became noticeably clear to me that these were gifts God placed in me to further The Kingdom. The funny part is that I was a little upset that I did not score higher in the area of evangelism because I had accepted my call to preach. What I did not know and understand at the time was that every preacher's pulpit is not in a church. My pulpit, for me, was board rooms and training rooms

E. CLAUDETTE FREEMAN

in the marketplace. And now, I use my gifts in the marketplace in a different capacity. The approach now is entrepreneurship using the same knowledge, gifts, talents, and abilities to consult and coach in the areas of professional and personal development. I have the freedom to use the methodologies or best practices based on biblical principles to help my clients.

My journey was not easy as I struggled with trying to balance work and ministry beliefs and concepts. I would find myself going far left or far right. I was either, so professional that I did not know how to truly see the needs of the people. Or I was too passive and allowed people to walk over me or get away with things they should have been disciplined for. Some of the struggles were a result of my own insecurities and a mentally and verbally abusive marriage that ended in divorce in 2008. Work-life-balance was difficult at that time. My faith was instrumental in keeping me from spiraling out of control. To add on to that, I had to deal with a great deal of envy and jealousy, and workplace haters. I have always been that person who was friendly, approachable, and greeted everyone with a huge sunshine smile. Yet, I believed in working hard and not using the workplace as a gossip hub.

As I continued to dive deeper into God's Word for solutions, it became evident that I was a light God was using in the marketplace to expose sin and corruption taking place in different organizations. I never entered into an organization intending to uncover or expose anything or anyone. Yet, my work ethics pushed me to do the right thing, and more importantly the God thing with boldness. The enemy made it exceedingly difficult for me, yet with God's favor, I always overcame, was promoted, or was moved on to a greater and better assignment. With every assignment, God always sent great mentors to help me grow.

One of my mentors gave me great advice that helped changed my mindset on how to communicate and build authentic personal relationships. He explained to me that at the end of the day, people really do not care how many degrees you have or how much you know. What they really want to know is how much you care. I took those words with me as I moved through Corporate America and now even more as a business owner. I made it a priority in every area of my life to focus on helping people, and not just monetary gain. Helping others is priceless, and it will always lead to blessings and favor you would have never imagined. I would have never gained any of this wisdom if I had not experienced brokenness in areas of my life. It is through my brokenness that God started to multiply me. I made the decision to move and operate in the gifts God gave me. I am a witness that your God given gifts will make room for you and bring you before great men.

For those who may struggle with not truly knowing what your gifts are, the first step is becoming self-aware. God made each one of us different and unique. Do not be comfortable with being a counterfeit when God designed you as an original masterpiece. Once you find your flow, get into it, and never allow anyone to disrespect your gifts. God give each one of us gifts to bless others and not ourselves.

Father God, I thank you for every gift, You have blessed me with to use in the marketplace. I submit all my business decisions and dealings to Your standards and declare that Your Word will be my guide and the foundation in all of my work. Amen.

PRAYER

Do It For His Name

Dr. Theresa Scott

> *"But as for you, be strong and do not give up, for your work will be rewarded." (Second Chronicles 15:7, NIV)*

> *"And whatever you do, whether in word or deed, do it all in the name of the Lord Jesus, giving thanks to God the Father through him." (Colossians 3:17, NIV)*

Heavenly Father, I enter into Your gates with thanksgiving and into Your courts with praise. I bless Your name. You are great and greatly to be praised. You are the King of glory, strong and mighty. You are mighty in battle. I give thanks to You for You are good and Your mercy endures forever.

Father, I come to You as Your creation in the Earth. I thank you for Your lovingkindness that You extend to me daily. You have blessed my life with gifts and abilities that could only come from You. These gifts and abilities have become my business in the Earth. This business is for the betterment of others. I ask You to grant me wisdom to provide the services and/or goods that accompany these gifts. Connect me to the right people who will benefit from it. I ask You to grant me favor with man to obtain all the necessary resources to maintain this business. Father open the way for my immediate supply to meet the demand for this splendid work. Let all that is mine by divine right now reach me in great avalanches of abundance so there will always be a surplus.

With Your help, this business will have a reputation for being operated with integrity, honesty, and fairness. I am committed to managing my affairs wisely so I can represent You well in the Earth. All that I have will be used for Your glory and honor. In Jesus' name, Amen!

Declaration:

I declare that the Spirit of the Lord is upon me. The spirit of wisdom, understanding, divine counsel, supernatural might, knowledge and of the fear of the Lord. I am divinely empowered and increase in skill and understanding. The Lord prospers the work of my hands.

PRAYER

Sealed in the Purpose of God

Evangelist Mozelle Mason

> *"Honor the LORD with your wealth, with the first fruits of all your crops." (Proverbs 3:9, NIV)*

Father, We come to you in the name of Jesus, the name that's above every name. The name to which every knee must bow, and every tongue must confess that You are Lord of Lord and Kings of Kings. we praise You and adore Your holy and righteous name because it is in You that we live, move, and have our very existence.

Oh Lord, Our God, we welcome your Holy Spirt into our place of business. we ask that You lavish Your blessings upon this business as it seeks to bring You glory in all its ways. we ask You to expand (name of business) and let it exemplify exemplary standards of service and integrity. Lord, we ask that Your favor rest upon every employee of this business and their families. we pray that those that enter our business sense Your presence, Your power, and Your love. Father we ask that You grant this business Your wisdom, favor, peace, success, and prosperity as we seek to honor You. We ask that Your Ministering Spirit clear the avenues for financial blessings to come forth from the north, south, east, and west. Father, as You bless this business, we will be careful to return portions of our income back to You according to Your Word in Malachi 3:10 and Proverbs 3:9.

According to Job 22:28, "Thou shalt also decree a thing, and it shall be established unto thee," therefore we decree and declare the following:

That this business and its employees shall glorify God in our daily operations.

That every employee will operate in the spirit of excellence as we seek wisdom daily from God.

That this business will meet its daily financial quota to cover operating expenses, future employee hires and benefits, new product development and projects.

That we will establish good customer relations with all we conduct business with.

We apply the blood of Jesus to every aspect of this business. We seal any and all partners (insert their names here) with Your blood and we bind every spirt of hinderance that will try to interfere with the success of this business (insert name here). In the mighty name of Jesus and for the glory of God. Amen.

Declaration:

I declare that the works of my hands will produce great and honorable things to the glory of God.

PRAYER

Bishop Michael Brennen

> *"Through faith we understand that the worlds were framed by the Word of God, so that things which are seen were not made of things which do appear." (Hebrews 11:3, KJV)*

> *"For the [a]overseer, as God's steward, must be blameless, not self-willed, not quick-tempered, not addicted to wine, not violent, not greedy for dishonest gain [but financially ethical]." (Titus 1:7, AMP)*

Oh, Creator God, You are The One who formed the universe and breathed life into all Your created beings, especially to humankind. We were made in Your image and likeness. You commanded us to be fruitful and to multiply in all the Earth. We thank you for the very spirit of our existence, and for the Divine command to procreate the world.

You have been our help, from the genesis of time to now. People plowed the fields, and You were there. While we kept livestock, You were our Great Shepherd. When we lost our way, You guided us back to the right path.

Throughout the ages You sent prophets and priests to encourage us in the paths of righteousness. And in the fullness of time, You sent your incarnate Son to redeem us to our full heritage as children of God. Therefore, as stewards of your creation, we pray for a full revelation that You have been our hope in ages past, and our hope for years to come.

The path has been difficult in recent years. The road has been stony with injustice and corruption, but we pray that we never mind the evil obstacles in the marketplace, but we pray that we uphold a standard of fairness in all our businesses. Many business owners have disregarded the environment - polluting and plundering the earth, uprooting indigenous people – but Lord we pray to be the sons and daughters of God that the whole creation is yearning for, like a mother in birth pangs, so that the entire world will be delivered from bondage.

We pray and believe that as the God of our weary years and silent tears, You will bring us into a new light to guide us into a new path of doing business. We thank you for the Holy Spirit that has indwelled us, protected us, provided for us, and leads us into all truth. We know You will be with us until the end of the ages. Therefore, we continue to praise and worship Your Divinity for this is our calling and destiny. Amen.

Declaration:

The integrity of my business is born from and rests in the integrity of God, always and in all ways.

YOUR CHARGE FOR
THE ASSIGNMENT

The Seven Disciples of Acts 6 and The Positions
They Call Forth in Business

E. Claudette Freeman

May I be fully transparent? I am going to lay a big card on
the table and in advance ask for your prayers. One of the most
daunting challenges I face as an entrepreneur is building a team
that fits the temperament, vision, mission, and purpose of the
company, as well as my quirkiness, personality, and temperament.
I have done far too much adjusting of me and the business to
accommodate rather than following the blueprint that had been
laid out for me.

I had to repent for that; especially considering God, in a time
of study, had given me the highlights of what should be on the
resumes of those I sought for the team. And a friend disclosed
that their company specifically asks that who they consider in a
human resources perspectives are asked specifically about their
walk with God and the intimacy of that relationship. You have
to fully line up with their spiritual beliefs to work with/for them.

God, the Master Steward, opened my eyes to the staff that a business steward should consider in Acts 6. It was one of those times of revelation with God when you are certain you are out in left field and may need a nap. But as I began to read, read, and read some more and then research those mentioned in that passage of scripture, not only did I discover potential job titles were there, but there was an understanding of the characteristics team members should embody.

I'm sharing this the way it unfolded for me and I trust that God will illuminate what you need.

1. Stephen means CROWN - the head, the leader, on the throne, full of faith and power. Not only should this be you as the entrepreneur; but it has to be the person who will serve directly next to or under you. This position is an Operations or Project Manager/Director.

2. Nicolas means VICTORY OF THE PEOPLE – my understanding is this is someone who gets the company's message across in a manner that supports the customer, but they can ensure what the people need is represented in a victorious manner by the company. This position is Client or Customer Relations, or Community Relations.

3. Philip means LOVER OF HORSES–in Biblical times those that owned horses were known to be wealthy/prominent and the name Philip is known to mean noble. This position then is related to integrity in manners of money and creating wealth, this type of person is ideal as a Financial Officer, Director of Finance, or Business Development Specialist.

4. Prochorus means LEADER OF THE DANCE – this name also is known to mean leader of the choir.

Prochorus became a Bishop later in his life. Since dance and music represent creativity and its importance in ministry - it seems since Prochorus succeeded in melding the arts with the spiritual. This position would be someone like an anointed Creative Director.

5. Nicanor means CONQUEROR – a conqueror is someone who overcomes the obstacles to succeed in battle and war, business growth is a consistent battle. This position seems to point to someone in Business or Operations Development. They are someone who can recognize the challenge and develop what is needed to conqueror it or find the programs, apps, or related to conqueror and implement it well.

6. Timon means HONORABLE/HONORING GOD – this position is an adjutant or assistant; this person must be honorable and integral above measure. Detailed in the weigh they show honor. This person would serve as an Administrative Assistant, Operations Assistant or Personal Assistant. They get the spirit of the business owner and the vision. This person might also be a Project Manager.

7. Parmenas means ENDURANCE/CONSTANCY in all matters – these are two characteristics that must be present in marketing, advertising, and promotions. This is someone who can study trends, estimate the longevity of an effort and the potential of results. This position describes in an Advertising Director, Marketing or Promotions Director.

You might read that passage of scripture and get a different revelation. That is wonderful. I think we should always engage scripture hoping and anticipating gleaning something more from it. In the meantime, as you consider what is laid out here, your challenge is to seriously and urgently identify what type of personnel (virtual or actual) your business requires. Even more important, weigh those who desire, or you seek to work in your business against the character of Christ and the character of those who He chose to serve with Him and why He made those choices. Cast your net wisely and intentionally.

<u>SCRIPTURES TO PONDER:</u>

Acts 6:1-8

DEVOTIONAL

THE WISDOM OF SOLOMON

Maxine Lloyd

> *"He has made everything beautiful in its time. Also, He has put eternity in their hearts, except that no one can find out the work that God does from beginning to end. I know that nothing is better for them than to rejoice, and to do good in their lives, and also that every man should eat and drink and enjoy the good of all his labor—it is the gift of God."*
>
> *(Ecclesiastes 3:11-13, NKJV)*

The Book of Ecclesiastes was written by King Solomon, the wisest man that ever lived. King Solomon, son of King David, became the ruler of all the tribes of Israel when he was just a young boy. You may ask, how would a young boy know how to take on such a great task and responsibility? No doubt, as his father, King David, was a follower of The One True God in Israel that gave King David tremendous success in his rule over Israel. King Solomon would have been taught the ways, wisdom, and power of The One True God, Elohim, The Creator, of all things. God Elohim is the Creator and Maker of the heavens and the Earth, and all the host of them. King Solomon had a magnificent work to rule, guard, and protect all of the twelve tribes of Israel.

These were not just any people, but God's chosen people, of whom He chose to reveal Himself.

It is in Genesis 1:1-31, the account of God speaking all of creation into existence. In the beginning before God created the heavens and Earth, the Earth was without form, and void; and darkness was on the face of the deep. God spoke, and said, "Let there be light;" and there was light (Genesis 1:2). God called the light day, and the darkness, He called night. So, the evening and the morning were the first day. And when creation was completed, God saw all that He had made, and indeed it was exceptionally good (vs. 30). When God finished his work, the evening and the morning were the sixth day (vs. 31). God's final creation on the sixth day was the creation of man. Man was put in a garden (Garden of Eden) to dress and to keep (Genesis 2:15). In the Hebrew, to dress means to work, and to keep is to guard or protect.

Understanding the creation story and knowing from the beginning of all time, God's Providence, Sovereignty, and Omniscience, established the purpose and mission of man to work, to rule, guard and protect all that God has made (Genesis 1:28). For King Solomon, who better to seek for wisdom on how to rule God's own people. Instead of riches, fame, and fortune, King Solomon asked for wisdom to carry out his work and responsibilities. As a result, God gave King Solomon, not only wisdom to be the wisest man that ever lived, but also God gave him riches, fame, and fortune.

Having purpose is to work and to serve for God's glory in everything we set our hands to do. We cannot find out the work that God does at any time. However, we know that the work He assigns for us is for our good and His glory. In all things, God acts first! God worked first for six days and then He rested. He set the standard of the work week and times. On the seventh day, God rested. Some call it the Sabbath; others call it Sunday (or

Saturday). Whatever you call it, God set the day as a day of rest and enjoyment to celebrate the work and service of your hands.

Who better to ask, what is your work and purpose? Who did God create you to be for His glory? Work was never meant to be tedious or hard, until the fall of man in the Garden of Eden, when man disobeyed God and sin entered into the world. The consequences of the fall caused the ground to be cursed and man to toil in his work for food. Sin brought death, but God had already prepared Himself a body, Jesus Christ, to bring life and salvation to all humanity. Accepting Jesus Christ, as Lord and Savior for the forgiveness of your sin, you become a member of God's family. You will have all the access, riches, and wisdom that come from the Holy Spirit that dwells in you through Jesus Christ. Like King Solomon, when we seek God for our life purpose, God can do so much more in you and through you for all eternity. Don't wait another day. Today is God's opportunity to work in your life.

> *"I must work the works of Him who sent Me while it is day; the night is coming when no one can work!"* (John 9:4, NKJV)

Abba Father, Today, I seek You for Your leading and guiding me into my work and purpose so that You are glorified. Bless the work of my hands that I will know You are with me. Amen.

AFFIRMATIONS

I will work with You as my partner, Lord. I work according to Your daily agenda and perform for an audience of one – the Lord Jesus Christ.

I accept the ministry, anointing and mantle that God has given me, and I speak every resource, dollar and other provision needed is manifesting now.

I dwell in my prophetic portion, I increase in substance, territories are enlarged on my behalf, and I prosper in the land in which I abide.

I am the greatness of God, assigned to steward a business at this time, and I will do even greater works because I can ask for the works and the provision in His name.

I am debt-free personally and corporately. Debt is an enemy to my existence, the existence of my business and my legacy and therefore I come against it with the excellent stewardship of Christ.

PRAYER

I Commit My Ideas to The Lord

Regina Griffin

> *"Commit to the Lord whatever you do, and he will establish your plans." (Proverbs 16:3, NIV)*

Dear Lord of all creation, merciful and gracious are You in all things. Marvelous are Your witty ideas and masterful ventures. Thank you for gifting me with business savvy. Around me there are many entrepreneurs and founders walking in Your presence and trusting in You to provide the blueprint. I pray that they are open to Your voice and Your plan, as I am also kneeled before You humble, ready, and willing.

I am filled with the Spirit of God that provides me wisdom and understanding in managing and leading my business. My designs speak life and reaffirm faith.

There are so many gifts distributed among us. Our services are evidence that the Lord is lovingly and consistently at work.

The same God, with all power, works within me and others. I am a vessel of light to shine and illuminate the darkness, the path, and the love of God.

I commit all my ideas and all my plans to You, The Most High. I trust in Your protection over all my contracts and all my opportunities. All my interactions are presented to You to establish Your plans and provide the provisions.

Lord, You are able to do more than I can ask or imagine.

I am strong and courageous. Fear will not prevent me from showing up and showing out in my business, for the Lord is with me wherever I go. I present my business to You and ask that Your will be done.

Declaration:

Lord, You have anointed me with business savvy to impact the world with Your gifts, love, and vision. Thank you for using me with purpose.

PRAYER

Declaring God Over My Workplace

Min. Anita Faye Wilson

> *"Therefore, he reasoned in the synagogue with the Jews and with the Gentile worshipers, and in the marketplace daily with those who happened to be there." (Acts 17:17, NKJV)*

Most gracious and omnipotent God our Father. The God of Abraham, Isaac, and Jacob. The God who made promises that are still in effect to this very day. The God who is all seeing, all-knowing, and ever flowing. We praise You for who You are and all that You have done. Your grace is so sufficient, and You sustain us through trials, tribulation, tests, and storms. I give honor to the King of kings and Lord of Lords who is the Author and the Finisher of my faith. I praise You for You are Jehovah Jireh, the provider of all of our needs. For You say in Your Word in Philippians 4:19 that You shall supply all my needs according to Your riches in glory by Christ Jesus. I am eternally grateful for the promises that You made to me all the way from Abraham through the order of Melchizedek. You have never made a promise that You have not kept.

I bless You for my business and insight; and the creative ability You have given me to obtain wealth. Your Word says in Deuteronomy 8:18, "You shall remember the Lord your God, for it is he who gives you power to get wealth, that he may confirm his covenant that he swore to your fathers, as it is this day." As I walk through this journey as a business owner, I pray that doors be opened, business ventures be sealed, and clients draw near. God give me divine direction and clarity and help me keep my mindset intact.

I come against the spirit of fear and doubt that would seek to rob me of my blessings. You gave me gifts that come without repentance. And I praise You God for giving me the insight to take my talents from gifts to skills. Father in heaven, help me to maintain my skills and to keep them in top-notch condition so that I can continue to grow my business and be an example and a light in a dark world.

I build all my hope and trust in You dear God, and I believe Your hand is on everything that I do. So, God, I give it all to You and I pray that Your will be done. I pray that this business impacts lives. I pray that this business blesses me so that I can be a blessing to others. I come against any foul demonic spirit that would attempt to infiltrate my business, my mind, my body, and my family and associates. I bind the enemy on every hand. I come against division and discourse among staff members. I speak unity and peace. I'm grateful for Your guidance. You have been a light unto my path, and I know that You are still with me and will be with me all the days of my life. Thank you for the privilege and opportunity to come before Your Throne of Grace. Thank you for receiving my petitions. And I know that You are at work on my behalf. You hold the power of the world in Your hands. You own the cattle on a thousand hills. There's nothing that I could ever want, need, or ask for that You cannot do because You are a God who can do ANYTHING but fail. I will praise You with every breath in my body for the rest of my days. It's in the matchless and most powerful name of Jesus that I pray this prayer and ask all things. Amen.

Declarations:

- I declare prosperity over my business. For it is You, oh God, who gives seed to the sower.

E. CLAUDETTE FREEMAN

- I declare clear direction in every business venture, for I know that my steps are ordered by You, Lord.

- I declare a peaceful workplace between staff and clients. A no confusion zone. For You are not the author of confusion.

- I declare a boldness in my spirit to walk through doors that have been closed in my face. For You, oh God, have not given me the spirit of fear, but of love power and a sound mind.

DEVOTIONAL

BRANDING THAT GLORIFIES GOD

Hillary Beth Koenig

Lord, You are light and truth and all that is good. Father, You created us to be Your image-bearers. We reflect on who You are, and what You've done, trusting in Your Word about who You say we are and what we are destined to do in Your name. May we constantly strive to reflect Your attributes as we live out our calling.

In Second Corinthians 6:18, You say, "And I will be a father to you, and you shall be sons and daughters to me." As Your children, we want to honor and glorify You as we reflect Your grace and truth; we want to constantly be growing to be like You, as a child imitates their parents constantly. Let us focus on the bigger picture of who we are in You as we make our living, participate in true community, and learn how to reach out to others in this world.

We know we cannot do this perfectly, or in our own strength, Lord. But we will continuously grow as we seek You; as Second Corinthians 3:18, "But we all, with unveiled face, beholding as in a mirror the glory of the Lord, are being transformed into the same image from glory to glory, just as from the Lord, the Spirit." This transparency of having an unveiled face is possible because of the freedom being forgiven means for our lives – and all our business dealings, as well.

When people say the name of our business, let them feel drawn to the character we show as we live out our lives because of who You are and what You've done through Your Son, Jesus Christ, on The Cross.

Ephesians 5:1 "Therefore be imitators of God, as beloved children; and walk in love, just as Christ also loved you and gave Himself up for us, an offering, and a sacrifice to God as a fragrant aroma."

It's been said that a company cannot be the best at everything; either they have the highest quality, or the lowest prices – the best customer service, or the best hours – the best variety, or the easiest store to navigate – and so on. But when a company strives to focus on their main goal, and also seeks to not completely neglect the other aspects of their business, they will truly stand out. You can think of several distinct brands, and what they are known for being the best at – so ask yourself, what do I want to be known for, when it comes down to the best thing about my company? Do that well, and as you make decisions, pause to evaluate how this all works into your brand's image.

There will always be aspects of a business that can improve and change over time, but a focus on the specific work and, culture, characteristics you want to be true of your company will result in written policies being carefully crafted, consequences for going against those specific actions and behaviors, and intentional conveying of and simultaneously living out those things every day in the workplace. You cannot expect those within your business to know what is expected of them if you are not intentional or demonstrating these things yourself! But you can set the standard for all to see and be held accountable, at every level, and start building a reputation of integrity. You cannot tolerate stealing, lying, sexual harassment, racism, putting others down in gossip, sabotaging the team, mocking customers, being dishonest in work dealings – and then expect to be known as a company that serves others well, can be trusted, or reflects the way we are to honor other image-bearers *(Genesis 1:27, "So God created mankind in his own image, in the image of God he created them; male and female he created them.")*.

People try to protect their reputations at great costs when they have done something wrong and know the truth being leaked might result in even greater losses for them. Often admitting a mistake when it is small prevents larger consequences. If you see something in your business going down a path that is not right, addressing the issue immediately will prevent future larger problems. It may even just be something that's getting outside of the main focus of your brand, and while not necessarily wrong, you cannot have your attention split in a million different directions; do what you do well, and don't try to hyperextend into all areas when you don't have the resources to go a certain direction, especially when through prayer you know what you need to do.

Let us each create a reputation that does nothing less than point to our Father in all things; let us be above reproach, humble and forgiving, kind and emphatic, and all the while standing strong in the truth. Father, help us cultivate a brand that stands out among the rest, representing the good in all things. Keep our focus on You in every choice that we make so that we build something that can glorify You. In Jesus' name. Amen.

PRAYER

Connecting to God's Anointed Resources

Dr. Theresa Scott

> *"Great is the Lord, and greatly to be praised; and his greatness is unsearchable. One generation shall praise thy works to another and shall declare thy mighty acts. I will speak of the glorious honour of thy majesty, and of thy wondrous works." (Psalm 145:3-5, KJV)*

Great are You Lord and Your greatness is unsearchable. You are gracious and full of compassion. Lord You are good to all, and Your tender mercies are over all Your works. O Lord most high You are a great King over all the Earth. You are my Redeemer. You are the First and the Last – the Alpha and Omega, and beside You there is no God.

Father, I bless You for Your goodness and Your mercy. Thank you for life, health, and strength. Thank you for being the Keeper of my soul for I realize that without You I can do nothing. I humble myself under Your rule and reign. You are my Lord and my God. I bless You for blessing me with the ability to do business in the Earth to help meet the needs of others. I value this business and commit it into Your hands. Grant me Your continual wisdom in the operation of it. I pray for favor with You and man. I only ask that You release to me that which is mine by divine right. You have designed this business for a particular group of people. Connect me with them and them with me. I thank you in advance for all the resources necessary to operate this business. May this business prove to be exactly what the people need. This is an honorable business representing The Kingdom of God. Ephesians 3:20 says You can do exceedingly abundantly above all that I may ask or think. Thank you in advance for increased abundance and profitability in this business. In Jesus' name, Amen!

"But remember the Lord your God, for it is he who gives you the ability to produce wealth, and so confirms his covenant." (Deuteronomy 8:18)

"I am the Lord your God, who teaches you what is best for you, who directs you in the way you should go." (Isaiah 48:17)

Declaration:

I am an irresistible magnet for all that belongs to me by divine right. The name of this business is being released in the atmosphere of those seek its goods and/or services. I declare that nobility and greatness is my portion.

PRAYER

Building a God Foundation

Evangelist Annette L. Anderson

"And he spake a parable unto them to this end, that men ought always to pray, and not to faint." (Luke 18:1, KJV)

Father in the name of Jesus, we thank you for all that You have done, for You have been good, wonderful and we thank you. May our God enable us to find peace and joy, as He guides our feet into the paths of His righteousness through the power of prayer. For prayer is an essential part our everyday life

Lord, I come to offer up prayer to You, as Your people begin to build and shape their new businesses. Please cover all investments and the people that we will need to encounter to help us further the business endeavors. I pray that our dealings are conducted in a manner that will please You. Help us to run these businesses efficiently, effectively, and God-centered. Teach us how to be a servant, first to You and the community that we serve. God when You open the doors of Your grace, please send the right people that will be an asset and not a liability to the business. God, please let people see You in all that we do, allow Your light to continuously shine for all to see. The Bible states, "Let your light so shine before men that they will see your good work and glorify the Father that is in heaven." (Matthew 5:16) Please allow us to be a beacon of light in our communities, churches, and the utter most parts of the world.

God, as our businesses begin to flourish, we ask for Your help to grow and become better people as business owners. If there is anything that's does not look like You in us, please remove it, so that You will truly get the glory. God, I pray in advance for innovative ideas and strategies, so that we will produce excellent and forward-thinking goods and services. I pray that everything that our hands touch will prosper. Deuteronomy 15:10 states, "… because that for this thing the Lord thy God shall bless thee in all thy works, and in all that thou puttest thine hand unto."

We understand that tactical planning will be required to build these businesses, so please endow us with the ability to learn all that we can, to provide top-notch service to our customers. We do understand that continued training is a necessity to run a successful business, so grant us what is needed to be to become the business owners You've called us to be. Father, our knowledge is limited, and we are flawed, but we know where our help comes from. Your Word says in Proverbs 1:7, "The fear of the Lord is the beginning of knowledge; fools despise wisdom and instruction." God, I am asking You to lead and guide us as we endeavor to follow Your footsteps and walk worthy of this calling. The Bible says in Psalm 37:23, "The steps of a good man are ordered by God." God give us the strength to not give up, even when the business does not appear to grow at the pace we have planned. Please allow us to keep going forward one step at a time.

Give us the strength to be able to withstand the darts of the enemy and his blows as the business grows. God please do not allow our insecurities to impede the blessings that You have given but give us the strength to continue the fight for our blessing. God, please give us hearts to give to others as you so richly bless us, to pour back into others. So, Father I thank you for the businesses that You have afforded each person, we will always be thankful to You for Your many blessings. God help us to put You first. We pray for our business and all those we will encounter. In the name of Jesus, amen.

Declaration:

When you are building a business, the Word of God is necessary to ensure it has the right foundation. Prayer is the cornerstone that should be laid.

DEVOTIONAL

THE CANAANITE WOMAN

Ebony Wilson

"Then Jesus went thence and departed into the coasts of Tyre and Sidon. And behold, a woman of Canaan came out of the same coasts, and cried unto him, saying, Have mercy on me, O Lord, thou son of David; my daughter is grievously vexed with a devil. But he answered her not a word. And his disciples came and besought him, saying, Send her away; for she crieth after us. But he answered and said, I am not sent but unto the lost sheep of the house of Israel. Then came she and worshipped him, saying, Lord, help me. But he answered and said, It is not meet to take the children's bread, and to cast it to dogs. And she said, Truth, Lord: yet the dogs eat of the crumbs which fall from their masters' table. Then Jesus answered and said unto her, O woman, great is thy faith: be it unto thee even as thou wilt. And her daughter was made whole from that very hour." (Matthew 15: 21-28, KJV)

This is the known story of the Canaanite woman. This passage of scripture plants us in the west Asian country of Lebanon and comes to life in the cities of Trye and Sidon. It is here that

E. CLAUDETTE FREEMAN

Jesus and his disciples are on a trip and barely arrive to their destination before they encounter the Canaanite woman. She had a basic request – for Him (Jesus) to heal her daughter from an evil spirit. I am sure we could all agree that by this time Jesus was l known to be a miracle worker and deliverer as well as for His other life altering encounters.

As the text continues, we are given a bird's eye view of the woman, the disciples, and Jesus' interactions. Jesus presumably ignores the woman as He tends to "the work at hand". The woman quickly moves on to petition the disciples who then ask Jesus to "please take care of her because she is driving us crazy." Jesus denies her a second time. The Canaanite woman being the incessant person she was did not allow a couple of unfavorable responses to deter her from the preferred outcome. She went to Jesus, dropped to her knees and begun to beg for Jesus' help. Again, Jesus denied her (this is the third time if you're keeping count), saying "it's not right to take bread out of the children's mouths and throw it to dogs." Now, let's take a moment to be honest here, if that same or a similar statement was directed toward you, you would move from a feeling of despair to a feeling of resentment. Full transparency, I would have completely missed my blessing because I would have allowed my emotions to get the best of me. I know I am not alone in this thought. But let's take some time to talk this through. The Canaanite woman jumped right into action and said: "You're right, Master…." It was at that moment in the text that I realized that there is a certain level of maturity that is required for progress to happen in our lives. Not only are we responsible for managing our emotions but being led by our emotions can erect barriers on the path set to achieve our preferred conclusion.

What you may have missed is that this encounter included the disciples, the woman, and Jesus. With that in mind understand that Jesus' response to her was as much for her as it was for the disciples. Jesus was teaching His disciples a lesson on priorities – remember He and the disciples were already tending to "the work at hand"- while simultaneously providing the woman an opportunity for personal growth to scale her faith. The Canaanite woman went on to say: "but beggar dogs do get scraps from the master's table." Jesus gave in. "'Oh woman, your faith is something else. What you want is what you get!' Right then her daughter became well." The Canaanite woman's humbling response coupled with the probable and unknowing support from the disciples catapulted her toward the response she believed was specifically ordained for her - the disciples only wanted Jesus to help her so that they could proceed with whatever their plans were for the day. Although the Canaanite woman was met with a delayed, exclusionary, and rude response, her reaction forever changed the trajectory of her life as she knew it.

> ➤ How do you respond in your business when you are opposed with resistance?
> ➤ Do you allow your emotions and the response of others to control the actions you take?
> ➤ What has this illustration of the Canaanite woman taught you about perspective in business?
> ➤ How will you scale your faith from where it is now?

I would venture to say that this woman exemplifies the tenacity that is missing from our lives. I can honestly say that there have been times when I prematurely quit. Maybe you, like me, have lost a lot-relationally, emotionally, physically, or spiritually. But this is the challenge you need to propel your faith to match a new perspective that will allow for you – us - to ask anything of God. I dare you to ask again, go again, try again and NEVER, under any circumstances accept anything less!

Let's pray! Generous and caring Father, I boldly ask that You lend Your ear to the person reading this prayer. Grant them the experiences, ability, and circumstances that will extend opportunities their way to ignite the desire to believe again. Give them the tenacity to allow the winds of life to elevate their faith. It is in Jesus' name we pray, amen!

PRAYER

I Commit, Submit and Surrender It To You

E. Claudette Freeman

> "Commit thy works unto the LORD, and thy
> thoughts shall be established." (Proverbs 16:3,
> KJV)

"And it shall come to pass, if thou shalt hearken diligently unto the voice of the LORD thy God, to observe *and* to do all his commandments which I command thee this day, that the LORD thy God will set thee on high above all nations of the earth: And all these blessings shall come on thee, and overtake thee, if thou shalt hearken unto the voice of the LORD thy God. Blessed *shalt* thou *be* in the city, and blessed *shalt* thou *be* in the field. Blessed *shall be* the fruit of thy body, and the fruit of thy ground, and the fruit of thy cattle, the increase of thy kine, and the flocks of thy sheep. Blessed *shall be* thy basket and thy store. Blessed *shalt* thou *be* when thou comest in, and blessed *shalt* thou *be* when thou goest out. The LORD shall cause thine enemies that rise up against thee to be smitten before thy face: they shall come out against thee one way and flee before thee seven ways. The LORD shall command the blessing upon thee in thy storehouses, and in all that thou settest thine hand unto; and he shall bless thee in the land which the LORD thy God giveth thee. The LORD shall establish thee a holy people unto himself, as he hath sworn unto thee, if thou shalt keep the commandments of the LORD thy God and walk in his ways.

> *And all people of the earth shall see that thou art*
> *called by the name of the LORD; and they shall*

be afraid of thee. And the LORD shall make thee plenteous in goods, in the fruit of thy body, and in the fruit of thy cattle, and in the fruit of thy ground, in the land which the LORD sware unto thy fathers to give thee. The LORD shall open unto thee his good treasure, the heaven to give the rain unto thy land in his season, and to bless all the work of thine hand: and thou shalt lend unto many nations, and thou shalt not borrow." (Deuteronomy 28:1-12, KJV)

Dear Lord, Sovereign God,

Your name is worthy to be praised. You are the King of kings and the Lord of lords. You alone are to be lifted high. I praise You for blessing me in the land that You have given me.

You have, You are, and You will open the storehouses of your bounty, the realms of heaven, to send rain in the land. Your Word says that You will bless the work of my hands according to Your will and assignment for me. I receive the blessing. I thank you for promising to increase the works of my hands, and for choosing the work of my hands to be in entrepreneurship. I receive that promise. I submit and surrender my business and every project, idea, vendor, staff member, partner, and opportunity to You, oh Jehovah.

I trust You to ignite wisdom, ignite ideas, and bring the clarity, provision, and resources I need to produce and be an excellent steward of a holistically prosperous business. Enlarge my territory, Jehovah Jireh, sustain me mightily as I cast every business and personal care on you so that I may be able to worship You without or even through hindrances and obstacles. Bless me to be a blessing. May my business be a vessel of charitable goodwill to administer to the needs of the widows/widowers, the least, the lost and left out.

Thank you for creating me for Your glory with a purpose and plan for my life. Thank you for the gifts and talents you have given me. Thank you for Your word which says I can do all things through You, because You strengthen me. Thank you for the promise that if I commit whatever I do to You, You will cause my plans to succeed. Father, thank you in advance for blessing my business Endeavors. Father you said if I walk in your ways and observe your commands, I will prosper in everything I do. I thank you

And now, God, my Savior, let my thoughts be Your thoughts, let Your Kingdom rest upon my business. It is in the matchless name of Your Son, Jesus, that I pray. Amen.

Declaration:

I decree and declare that I operate in the excellent stewardship of Christ and as I excel in Him, I excel in the prosperity, prominence, and purpose of my business.

AFFIRMATIONS

I possess a Kingdom paradigm, which grants me new ways of thinking, new ways of working and new ways of living.

New cycles of victory, success and prosperity are replacing old cycles of failure, poverty, and death in my life.

My life, my spirit, my heart energy are intertwined in the energy of the Christ and therefore that energy brings to me by my presence in heavenly and earthly places all manners of prosperity, provision, and resources.

Because of the anointing and what God has called me to do, sponsors, clients and the like seek me out and desire to do business with all things associated and attached to me.

I wear the helmet of salvation to protect my mind from negative thoughts that would derail Your purposes and plans for me. Truth protects my integrity, righteousness protects my reputation, the gospel of peace guides my every step, the shield of faith secures my future and destiny, and the sword of The Spirit grants me dominion and authority in every venue.

PRAYER

Confidence in God

Britany A. Brooks

> *"Now behold, today I am going the way of all the earth, and you know in all your hearts and in all your souls that not one word of all the good words which the LORD your God has promised concerning you has failed; all have been fulfilled for you, not one of them has failed." (Joshua 23:14, AMP)*

Most Gracious and Loving Father,

We give You all the honor and all the glory, for even when the seasons change, You remain the same. Lord, You are our God; we will exalt You and praise Your name, for in perfect faithfulness You have done wonderful things planned long ago.

Father, we thank you for the intelligence, the knowledge, and the craftsmanship You've bestowed upon us through The Holy Spirit. For it's through Your Spirit we are able to educate, to heal, to restore, and to continuously be a light in this desolate world. Lord, it's because of You; we will lack no good thing. For "every good and perfect gift is from above, coming down from the Father of the Heavenly lights." (James 1:17) What a blessing it is to know that the gifts You've given us, will make a difference in this world. We will overcome this world! For You have overcome this world, and greater is He that is within Your children; than he that is within the world! (First John 4:4)

Father, though these times are uncertain; and the journey will not be easy. You've still given us a way out. A way that's not temporary or short term, but a way that's sealed in Your permanence. You have given the way through Your Word! So, Lord, may Your children keep Your Word imprinted on their hearts. For Your Word says, "For I know the plans I have for you, plans to prosper and not to harm you; plans to give you hope and a future." (Jeremiah 29:11) And so, Lord, we know You didn't call us into marketplace ministry without a plan to prosper us! Our King, You wouldn't have given us a mind to establish creative ideas and designs, without a plan to sustain them! So, whatever is done, whether in word or deed, may it all be done in the name of the Lord Jesus, giving thanks to God the Father through Him. Lord, You've made us to be Your handiwork, who were created in Christ Jesus to do Your good works. So may we never become weary in doing good. For at the proper time, we will reap a harvest if we do not give up. (Galatians 6:9)

"And my God will meet all your needs according to the riches of his glory in Christ Jesus." (Philippians 4:19)

Lord God, You are not man that You should lie, and You are not human that You should change Your mind! And so, this is the confidence we have in You, that You will act on Your promises!

Father, this is the confidence we have in You, that You will not lead Your children to failure. As scripture says, "Anyone who believes in Him will never be put to shame." (Romans 10:11) "Therefore, everyone who hears these words of mine and puts them into practice is like a wise man who built his house on the rock. The rain came down, the streams rose, and the winds blew and beat against that house; yet it did not fall, because it had its foundation on the rock." (Matthew 7:24-27) So, Lord, even when the storm comes, our works will not crumble; for they were built on the

ETERNAL ROCK! All glory to the only wise God through Jesus Christ, forever! Amen.

Declaration:

I declare healing and restoration through the works of my ministry. I declare growth in wisdom and in my area of expertise. I declare by the Spirit of the True and Living God, a prosperous future!

YOUR CHARGE FOR THE ASSIGNMENT

A Widow Set to Die and Abundance

E. Claudette Freeman

In First Kings 17, the prophet Elijah, after spending time at the brook of Cherith, has been sent by God to encounter a widow in Zarephath. He meets this woman as she is gathering sticks and asks her for water and bread. She tells him she has no bread. Further, she advises him that she was gathering sticks to take the little flour and little oil that she had in her home to create a final meal for she and her son. It would be the last thing they ate before they died.

Elijah convinced her to do otherwise as we read in verses 13-15 (NIV): "Elijah said to her, "Don't be afraid. Go home and do as you have said. But first make a small loaf of bread for me from what you have and bring it to me, and then make something for yourself and your son. For this is what the Lord, the God of Israel, says: 'The jar of flour will not be used up and the jug of oil will not run dry until the day the Lord sends rain on the land.'" She went away and did as Elijah had told her. So, there was food every day for Elijah and for the woman and her family. [16] For the jar of flour was not used up and the jug of oil did not run dry, in keeping with the word of the Lord spoken by Elijah."

The entrepreneur can find strategy and encouragement in this passage of scripture. If we look at it through the eyes of the concerned business owner, our overall business or corporate understanding is this – God will take the very last that we have

AND our weakness, apply His Word to it so that the jar of flour and the jug of oil will not run dry.

Where is the strategy in this passage? Read on. In verses 10-11, the woman was gathering sticks for that last meal. We find ourselves in that place as owners/stewards of a business sometimes. We decide we are going to finish that project, not take on any more clients and take the sign down and lock the doors permanently. We have just enough for that final week or month.

Yet, when the prophet (a STRANGER to her) asked for water and bread, she obliged, although a little coaxing was necessary. What we learn in this is that we should give even when we've decided to give up; and we should serve - even a stranger - because they may be bringing the things or resources or move of God we need.

In verses 11-14 we note that the prophet did not tell her to stop what she was doing, instead He said several things we should not miss.

(1) Pause and serve me before you continue. He did not stop her from her plan because he was aware that she needed to see a powerful move of God in her situation and in the drought around her. Still his request was SERVE.

(2) He encouraged her to do what she was going to do but with a different understanding and mindset. He dared her to believe that since she was serving someone in need, what was a moment of giving up was about to become the opportunity to be provided for.

(3) The prophet told her that the flour and oil - grace and anointing - of the provision of The Lord for her house (in this case our businesses) would flow until The Lord sent rain to the Earth. Which means her sufficient

E. CLAUDETTE FREEMAN

provision would flow immediately and would increase when the rain came and allowed the crops, the grain, the livestock in the region to flourish again. Look again, there is provision in your barren vessels (opportunities).

(4) The sufficient provision God provides can become abundant provision. We see this not only with this widow but with the widow in Second Kings 4, when the oil flowing through the vessels her sons gathered not only covered her debt but provided enough for she and her sons to live on.

(5) Have a purpose and a vision for what you have (even the last of it). Things sometimes look bleak, even dead, but it is our attention to the Word of God that makes a difference. If we seek His Kingdom first and take care of His people through our assignment, then we posture ourselves for abundant provision.

(6) While on your course, listen for a word, a new concept, a unique variation, or an innovative idea that will not come from a voice you know but a voice you should know. The widow's assurance was not in the prophet, but in whom she believed sent him.

(7) There is something else that spoke volumes to me in this passage. The widow was OUT GATHERING sticks – the resources she needed to carry out her mission. Where are you gathering? Trust God, heed The Word and get out of your comfort zone, your familiar territory and go where the resources are to gather them unto you.

God did something for this widow that I unequivocally believe He can do in each of our businesses – resurrect it in times of struggle and downturns; and use the shift for our good and His glory.

SCRIPTURES TO PONDER:

I Kings 17:1-15

II Kings 4:1-7

DEVOTIONAL

COMMIT YOUR WORKS

Pastor Pamela Shaw

"Commit your works to the Lord, and your thoughts will be established." Proverbs 16:3

I remember the first time I dropped my oldest son off to his grandmother's house while I went to work. He was a little over a year old and it was my first time away from him since he was born. Even though he was in the very capable hands of family, I was still nervous. For nine months, I carried this little developing person in my womb. I was his life-source until his birth. After being born, I was the central part of furthering his development and still remained a life-source for him. It was a blessing being there for him during that entire first year of his life. Watching him complete first-year milestones made me a little skeptical about leaving him once it was time for me to go to work. What other milestones would I miss? How would he react when I left him for the day? Does my dependence on someone else to care for my child deem me a bad mother? Those were the questions I struggled with as I handed off my not-so-little bundle and kissed him good-bye on that first day. He had a great first day. He had a great second day. He had a great third day. He had a great first week. It just took my total trust.

When the seed of your business was planted and it began to formulate, you were the life-source to its development during those preliminary stages. The intricate parts of its beginning stages were in your very capable hands, and you watched it take shape and form into an entity that would have its place in the world. But even in all that you did, there are still areas and places in which further development could happen. Those areas may require you to turn your baby over to someone else for insight, expansion or just to ease your load. I'm sure the questions start forming or doubts about your abilities start to play out in your mind, you did birth this now formed seed. But just like I was with my firstborn, you want what you've brought to life to develop and grow into something great. And no matter how much I continued to put my hand in, on, over and around him, there were areas that were beyond my personal scope. I had my own personal limits. My tastes were different, so until my son was put into his grandmother's care, there were certain foods he would have never been introduced to if he were solely with me. I know there were certain ways he would have been short-sighted in viewing the world around him if he and I were only subject to my limited areas of travel. I also realized there were certain relationships that would not have been established as well. As much as I wanted to be his everything, at all times, in every way, it wasn't possible. I had to put my trust of his care into someone else's hands and although it was hard to let go, it proved to be valuable to his growth overall.

This is no different when you commit your works to the Lord. He is The One who can take your business into places and areas of growth and expansion that your hand and vision alone cannot reach. He is The One that releases the favor that will cause relationships to come together, working things out for your good. Where you may find yourself short-sighted in an area, He is The One that will cause you to see in ways and areas far beyond your natural eye. You just have to totally trust Him to take absolute

E. CLAUDETTE FREEMAN

care of your baby. He is able to do exceedingly, abundantly, above all you can ask or think according to the power that works in you. He will make the very works of your hands firmly established and prosperous.

Father, thank you for this business that I commit it into Your very capable hands. As You lead and guide me, I thank you in advance for remarkable success each step of the way. In Jesus' name, Amen.

PRAYER

May We Not Get Comfortable in Complacency

Metris Batts-Coley

> *Therefore, preparing your minds for action, and being sober-minded, set your hope fully on the grace that will be brought to you at the revelation of Jesus Christ. (Peter 1:13, ESV)*

> *"Ask, and it will be given to you; seek, and you will find; knock, and it will be opened to you." (Matthew 7:7, ESV)*

> *"Do not let your hearts be troubled. You believe in God; believe also in me." (John 14:1, NIV)*

Gracious God, my Lord, thank you for another day of life and breath. May we take time to focus on the small steps and the little things that will lead us in the right direction. Let us think before we do and become aware of our actions and reactions to the steps we make. May we receive Your grace and mercy as a blessing as we learn the lessons of life. May we realize that trial and error make practice perfect.

Today, Lord, let me be open to asking for help. Don't let what I cannot do; get in the way of what I can. And God, may I never allow doubt or distrust to interfere with, hinder or deny what You can do. Turn my stumbling blocks into steppingstones of glory. Remind me Lord that I get and stay stuck because I don't ask for help. I limit my abilities by not asking for help or identifying my needs before You.

Lord help me move beyond my earthly fears because fear and faith cannot live in the same heart. Help me God trust You in ways that stretch my faith, which encourage me to walk through the fire, which dare me to walk with an Almighty Savior who cannot fail with boldness.

Gracious God, let us not spend time on idle things while Your assignment and calling for us goes undone. May we not be comfortable, complacent, or fine with the status quo. May we never be afraid of new challenges or fearful of what's behind the next door. Let today's lessons in my business and all that we do build our confidence and help us to become overcomers. May the love of Jesus seal these words. It is in His name, we pray. Amen!

Declaration:

I am in the trusted Hands of God; I cannot fail.

DEVOTIONAL

NO FEAR IN GOD'S BUSINESS

By Regina Griffin

Second Timothy 1:7 states "For God has not given us a spirit of fear but of power and love and sound mind."

Peace, love, and blessings to all of God's amazing children. The power of God is before you, ever present, loving, and consistent. God gives us the gift of eternal love and light. God's Word is steadfast and clear. God's Word gives us a spirit of power, love, and self-discipline and we are GLAD ABOUT IT!

What is fear? Well, it depends on who you ask. Fear is defined as "an unpleasant emotion caused by anticipation or awareness of danger." When we interact with new clients, apply for business credit, launch a new product we are sometimes faced with fear. Fear comes from the anticipation of a negative outcome. God's Word tells us otherwise! God's Word tells us over and over that He loves us and that His plans are to prosper and not harm us. God didn't give us the spirit of fear. God's Word gives us the confidence of knowing that even when we think we've made a mistake, even when a door is closed before us, even when we don't get the loan approval or land the new account God's Word is clear! He loves us unconditionally, and these setbacks are actually set-ups for blessing like we've never seen or could have imagined.

God's love should be displayed in all that we do, say, and to those we come in contact with. His love never departs from us and should be clear, present, and evident in our personal and professional lives. God's love should be displayed even to those that we cannot readily see any benefit to loving. God's love should be displayed even to clients, customers, vendors, etc. even if they are not kind or loving to us, because God is love.

Lord, we come to You as humbly as we know how, our lives, our families, our businesses, we owe all of our successes to You. We thank you for Your continued gift of life in such uncertain times. Lord, we know that even in the toughest of times on the darkest of nights that You are with us. We thank you for the protection of Your Word and stand firm on Your promises. Lord, we know that no matter what we face, Your Word says that it will be for our good. Lord, we thank you for all that You do, for fighting the battles and blessings both known and unknown. Lord, Your Word says, "For God has not given us the spirit of fear, but of power, and love, and sound mind." (Second Timothy 1:7)

Lord, I pray that we continue to remember Your Word as we go forth in our daily lives and business ventures. I pray that we remember to take You with us in all that we do. We ask these blessings in Your son Jesus name. Amen!

DEVOTIONAL

CHANGES IN THE MARKET

Hillary Beth Koenig

As the Creator of all things, God, You designed not only the smallest organisms, but also every system and process by which life exists and coexists in each ecosystem in this world. You created individuals unique within those systems, and as humans, we have the knowledge that we are not in control of these systems. By our nature, we tend to be afraid of what we cannot control. Let us reject giving into fear and instead praise You for being on the throne, active and working in our lives.

As we seek You, Father, Creator of our passions, we dedicate our talents, goals, and ventures to You. Every step of the way, may we recognize that we don't know what tomorrow brings, and entrust You with the future.

We know that James 4:13-15 says, "Now listen, you who say, 'Today or tomorrow we will go to this or that city, spend a year there, carry on business and make money.' Why? You do not even know what will happen tomorrow. What is your life? You are a mist that appears for a little while and then vanishes. Instead, you ought to say, 'If it is the Lord's will, we will live and do this or that.'"

E. CLAUDETTE FREEMAN

Let us not be dismayed in our trials and ever-changing circumstances, but ever seeking You, as it says also in James 1:5-6, "If any of you lacks wisdom, you should ask God, who gives generously to all without finding fault, and it will be given to you. But when you ask, you must believe and not doubt, because the one who doubts is like a wave of the sea, blown and tossed by the wind."

Recognizing our lack of control, and that You are all-knowing, all-powerful, and have the ability to be present everywhere all at once, we submit to Your loving guidance.

Second Corinthians 5:7 *"For we walk by faith, not by sight."*

Despite the best modeling, every year, from June first through November 30th, hurricane season comes to the coastal regions of the U.S. and many other countries. While building codes try to protect more recently constructed homes, and mandatory evacuations try to protect the vulnerable, and plywood boards go up on windows, when the store has run out of bottled water and you don't have any more canned soups, the desperation comes in, and some compromise - stealing, being ugly about resources, being bitter about lack of electricity, etc. Some have greater losses than others. Besides residential homes being impacted, businesses also feel the effects of damages, losses, and even sometimes result in long-term or final closure.

Thankfully, many individuals and businesses choose to help others in these times, spreading blue tarps over holes in roofs, clearing tree debris from yards, and volunteering to pass out relief food, water, and supplies. They see the needs in their community and decide to do whatever they can to meet those needs. As Christians in these types of situations, there are opportunities to be the hands and feet of Jesus, demonstrating perseverance even in frustrating circumstances.

In many ways similarly, when COVID-19 hit in 2019, no one really foresaw the impact it would have on how people would work, or that job pauses would become losses, stores would not being able to source certain products because of material shortages, school-aged kids would be unable to attend in-person classes for varying lengths of time, etc. It was up to each person, business owner, and school district to figure out how to make things work, and numerous businesses and individuals suffered from drastic, sudden changes.

While not every year brings a major disaster, no matter why the changes come about, or what the market changes are, you can have the peace of knowing that "in all things God works for the good of those who love him, who have been called according to his purpose," (Romans 8:28). Whether we face uncertainty, a negative change, or a positive one, we can remain steadfastly seeking the Lord in each situation for wisdom, support, strength, foresight, and the ability to grow into the person He created each of us to be, as we go about our business. When we put Him first and obey His laws, we ensure the circumstances surrounding us are not more of a driving factor than our focus on seeking justice, loving mercy, and walking humbly with the Lord (Micah 6:8).

I will remain at peace because my hope is in the Lord and not in the things of this world.

Father, I ask that You give me guidance in each of my steps, so that You may be glorified all along my path. When everything around me seems unstable or constantly changing, let me lean on You, The One whose promises are always true. In Jesus' name, I pray. Amen.

MY CORPORATE BOARD MEETING WITH GOD, REVELATION AND MORE

Our publisher, years ago, started holding monthly board meetings with God. It became her way of creating intentional space for she and God to plan, strategize, correct, and envision. Her board meeting time includes fasting two to three days before the scheduled meeting, a time of praise and worship, prayer and then she pulls out her agenda (which includes blank lines to allow God to add His discussion points). During the meeting, item-by-item she discusses what her victories, concerns and challenges are in the business. Then, during a time of exhortation, she listens for God to provide scriptures. Those scriptures are then studied and The Most High is asked to reveal how she should apply what's been read.

The areas in this book titled **YOUR CHARGE FOR THE ASSIGNMENT** are taken from her board meeting minutes!

Try it. Use this space to map out your agenda. List the things that you most need to hear God's direction on and determine when your monthly meetings will occur and what their format will be.

MY CORPORATE BOARD MEETING WITH GOD AGENDA

Date:_____

Called to order:_____

i.   Worship and Exhortation

ii.   Opening Prayer

iii.   _____

iv.   _____

v.   _____

vi.   _____

vii. _____

viii. _____

ix.   _____

x.   _____

xi.   _____

xii. Closing Prayer

NOTES FROM MY CORPORATE BOARD MEETING WITH GOD

Date:_____

SCRIPTURES ILLUMINATED:

_____
_____
_____
_____
_____
_____
_____
_____

GOD SPOKE:

_____
_____
_____
_____
_____
_____
_____
_____

MY NEXT STEPS:

_____
_____
_____
_____
_____
_____
_____
_____
_____
_____
_____
_____
_____
_____
_____
_____
_____
_____
_____
_____
_____
_____
_____
_____
_____
_____
_____
_____
_____
_____

E. CLAUDETTE FREEMAN

_____

_____

_____

_____

_____

_____

_____

_____

_____

_____

_____

_____

_____

_____

_____

_____

_____

_____

_____

_____

_____

_____

_____

_____

_____

_____

WRITE THE VISION

Habakkuk chapter two verse two tells us we should make our vision clear, we should write it down, and we should run with it. It is also wise to revisit your original vision statement occasionally for God's fine-tuning of it, to assure it's in line with business progression, and to determine if the vision has outgrown you or you've lost sight of it.

A solid vision statements clearly defines what you seek to accomplish; it gives you and those who might collaborate with you, aspirations or something that can be grasped as the big picture, comes from the leader with the understanding that those that run with it must lead in their respective areas. The vision statement should also include a number. In example, our vision is to become a recognized brand servicing more than 1500 customers per month in the tri-state area in our quest to become a Top 50 company by the end of the next calendar year.

Write the vision and make it clear

_____
_____
_____
_____
_____
_____
_____
_____
_____
_____
_____
_____
_____
_____
_____
_____
_____
_____
_____
_____
_____
_____
_____
_____
_____
_____
_____
_____
_____
_____
_____
_____

_____

_____

_____

_____

_____

_____

_____

_____

_____

_____

_____

_____

_____

_____

_____

_____

_____

_____

_____

_____

_____

_____

_____

_____

_____

_____

_____

_____

_____

_____

_____

WRITE THE MISSION

A mission statement is a thread that sews into your vision statement. The mission statement gives an abbreviated view of the company's purpose, and the reason for existing within the parameters of its line of business. The mission statement should motivate people to invest in human, financial or in-kind resources. With all of that in mind, note that this statement is two to three short sentences long.

What is the mission of your business?

_____
_____
_____
_____
_____
_____
_____
_____
_____
_____
_____
_____
_____
_____
_____
_____
_____
_____
_____
_____
_____
_____
_____
_____
_____
_____
_____
_____
_____
_____

_____
_____
_____
_____
_____
_____
_____
_____
_____
_____
_____
_____
_____
_____
_____
_____
_____
_____
_____
_____
_____
_____
_____
_____
_____
_____
_____
_____
_____
_____

MY PRAYER FOR MY BUSINESS

_____

_____

_____

_____

_____

_____

_____

_____

_____

_____

_____

_____

_____

_____

_____

_____

_____

_____

_____

_____

_____

_____

_____

_____

_____

E. CLAUDETTE FREEMAN

MY WEEKLY FAST

Fasting, when added to intentional prayer, is a powerful tool to gain God's desire, direction, covering, increased anointing and so much more.

As stewards of businesses, fasting is critical to assure that you are developing products and services that are wonderfully pleasing to The Father, able to transcend a myriad of woes, dogmas, disbelief and more to open a door for ministry, encouragement, and life transformation, and able to serve the communities in the areas where you conduct business.

Hopefully this sheet will allow you to dig in and turn down, turn off and release something to gain more of The Holy Spirit.

Day/Date:_____

Fasting about: _____
_____
_____
_____

Focus scriptures: _____
_____
_____
_____

What God spoke:

_____
_____
_____
_____
_____
_____
_____
_____
_____
_____
_____
_____
_____
_____
_____
_____
_____
_____
_____
_____
_____
_____
_____
_____
_____
_____
_____
_____
_____
_____
_____

MY WEEKLY FAST

Fasting, when added to intentional prayer, is a powerful tool to gain God's desire, direction, covering, increased anointing and so much more.

As stewards of businesses, fasting is critical to assure that you are developing products and services that are wonderfully pleasing to The Father, able to transcend a myriad of woes, dogmas, disbelief and more to open a door for ministry, encouragement, and life transformation, and able to serve the communities in the areas where you conduct business.

Hopefully this sheet will allow you to dig in and turn down, turn off and release something to gain more of The Holy Spirit.

Day/Date:_____

Fasting about: _____
_____
_____
_____

Focus scriptures: _____
_____
_____
_____

What God spoke:

_____
_____
_____
_____
_____
_____
_____
_____
_____
_____
_____
_____
_____
_____
_____
_____
_____
_____
_____
_____
_____
_____
_____
_____
_____
_____
_____
_____
_____
_____

_____
_____
_____
_____
_____
_____
_____
_____
_____
_____
_____
_____
_____
_____
_____
_____
_____
_____
_____
_____
_____
_____
_____
_____
_____
_____
_____
_____
_____
_____
_____
_____

MY WEEKLY FAST

Fasting, when added to intentional prayer, is a powerful tool to gain God's desire, direction, covering, increased anointing and so much more.

As stewards of businesses, fasting is critical to assure that you are developing products and services that are wonderfully pleasing to The Father, able to transcend a myriad of woes, dogmas, disbelief and more to open a door for ministry, encouragement, and life transformation, and able to serve the communities in the areas where you conduct business.

Hopefully this sheet will allow you to dig in and turn down, turn off and release something to gain more of The Holy Spirit.

Day/Date:_____

Fasting about: _____
_____
_____
_____

Focus scriptures: _____
_____
_____
_____

What God spoke:

E. CLAUDETTE FREEMAN

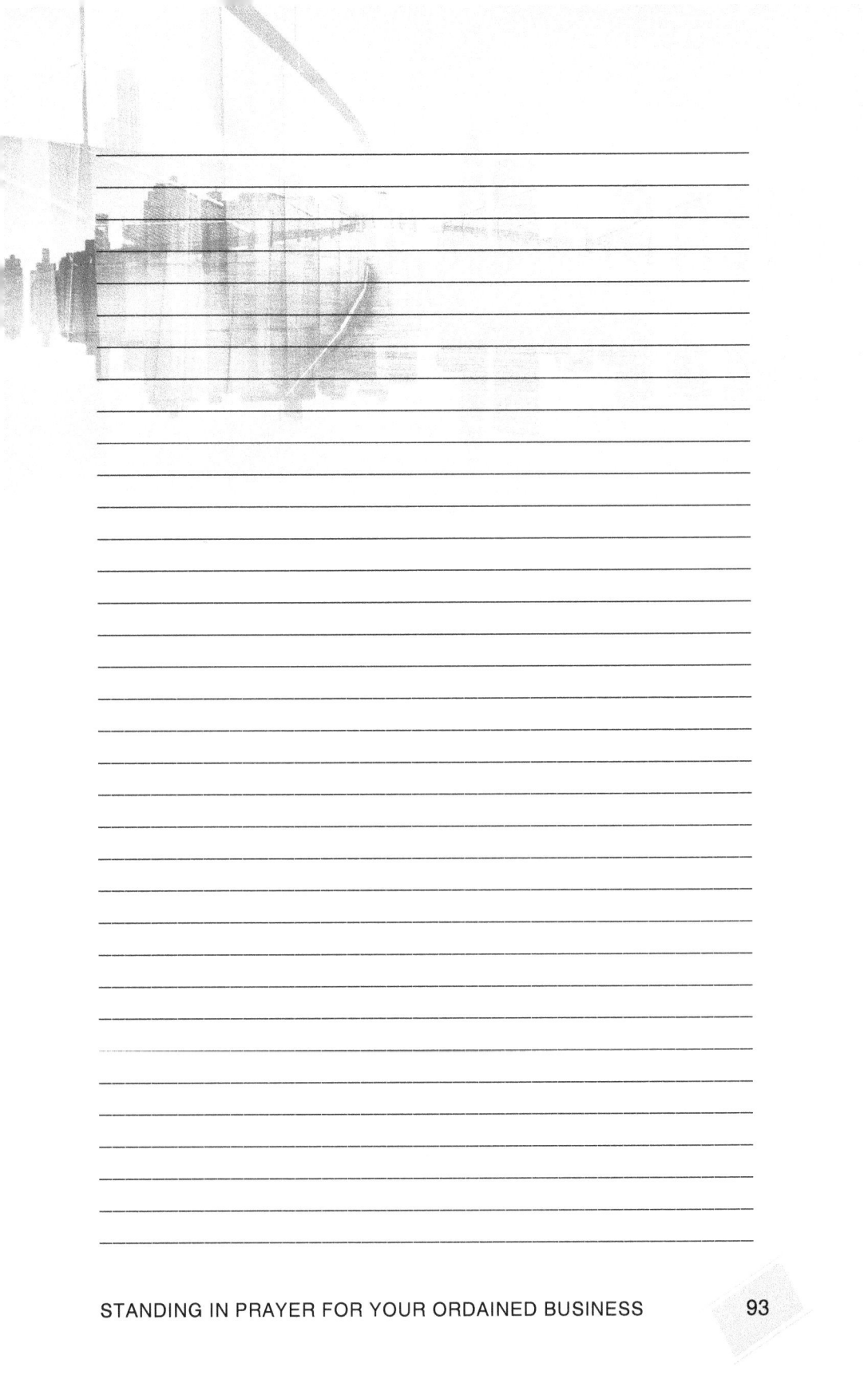

MY WEEKLY FAST

Fasting, when added to intentional prayer, is a powerful tool to gain God's desire, direction, covering, increased anointing and so much more.

As stewards of businesses, fasting is critical to assure that you are developing products and services that are wonderfully pleasing to The Father, able to transcend a myriad of woes, dogmas, disbelief and more to open a door for ministry, encouragement, and life transformation, and able to serve the communities in the areas where you conduct business.

Hopefully this sheet will allow you to dig in and turn down, turn off and release something to gain more of The Holy Spirit.

Day/Date:_____

Fasting about: _____
_____
_____
_____

Focus scriptures: _____
_____
_____
_____

What God spoke:

_____
_____
_____
_____
_____
_____
_____
_____
_____
_____
_____
_____
_____
_____
_____
_____
_____
_____
_____
_____
_____
_____
_____
_____
_____

_____
_____
_____
_____
_____
_____
_____
_____
_____
_____
_____
_____
_____
_____
_____
_____
_____
_____
_____
_____
_____
_____
_____
_____
_____
_____
_____
_____
_____
_____
_____
_____

CLOSING DECLARATION

Child of God,

Remain focused on truth and grace as you brand and build your business. Be fearless and confident in all aspects of your personal and professional life. Let integrity, truth, empathy, compassion, purpose, divine will, and a desire to minister through your business be your portion.

No matter what changes occur in the market, no matter what changes occur in your finances or in your human or other resources, allow trust and faith in God to be your strong towers.

May peace and prosperity be found in the fact that your security and your hope is in Christ alone.

E. Claudette Freeman

THE CONTRIBUTORS

Dr. Theresa Scott is a prophet, teacher, and empowerment speaker. She has been saved over 40 years. She ministers with her husband (Apostle Dr. Richard Scott) at Grow in Grace Worship Center, Delmar, Maryland. (www.gigwc.com). Dr. Scott received her Doctor of Divinity degree from Spirit of Truth Institute, Richmond, VA, Master of Christian Education and Bachelor of Biblical Studies degrees from H. E. Wood Bible Institute & Theological Seminary, Alexandria, VA. Dr. Scott is the author of PERFECTING MOMENTS and THE JOURNEY.

Regina Griffin was born and raised in Meridian, Mississippi, she is a mother of three. Her loves include writing in diverse styles, and technology including cybersecurity and programming. Regina is an avid believer in expressing love, living a positive lifestyle, encouraging others, and applying knowledge that impacts others, not only self. She can be found blogging, reading, tinkering with technology, enjoying family, and cooking up creative ideas to soothe her entrepreneurial spirit.

Pastor Pamela Shaw is a native of Richmond, Virginia. She has been married to Omar Shaw for twenty years and together they have five children. Pamela enjoys spending time with her family, reading, writing, singing, and acting. While being on the stage has been a life changing, saving grace for her, Pamela thoroughly enjoys directing as well. She is thankful for her start at Virginia Repertory Theatre and grateful for her growth at The Heritage Ensemble Theatre Company. She is the founder and pastor of 4th Wall Love Connect Ministries, an outreach ministry where she has been serving since 2017. Pamela is the Executive Administrative Manager of Pivot with P.A.M. Pivot Administrative Management™, a virtual administrative consultant business.

Rev. Maxine Lloyd Ball, MDIV, MSPC, LGPC is a Pastor and Licensed Graduate Professional Counselor providing psychotherapy integrative spirituality to victims of crime and treats other mental health concerns. She is passionate about God and His Word (Jesus). Rev. Maxine is blessed with the gifts of teaching and preaching to bring salvation to all who would receive Jesus Christ as Lord. She is the author of I'm Mad as at Hell, A Journey to Sanctified, Satisfied, and Single – Understanding the Dynamics of Domestic Violence and Spiritual Warfare. Her second book release, SCARS – The Roadmap to the Soul will be in bookstores soon.

Sarita Price resides in Memphis, TN. She is a mother, an author, adjunct professor, board certified life and leadership coach, and entrepreneur whose vision is to connect present and future leaders through innovative life and leadership coaching, talent development, and empowerment. Sarita wrote and published her first book Healing Through & From Sarita's Pen in 2014. Sarita is also co-author of an anthology entitled Tying the Knot Between Ministry and The Marketplace published April 2018. Sarita is a licensed and ordained preacher. You can connect with Sarita on social media at https://linktr.ee/fromsaritaspen.

Hillary Beth Koenig has been a freelance editor and writer for over a decade, beginning with editing devotionals for a Christian teen girls' website. As the wife of a service member, and mother of two, she is always finding new opportunities to build community and connect with others. Supporting small businesses, nonprofit organizations, and individuals in their written endeavors is a great honor for her.

Ebony Wilson is the founder of She's Poised: A Creative Services Co., a company that exists to - Brainstorm. Execute. Elevate. - alleviate unnecessary stress to optimize business productivity. Additionally, Ebony has experience in community mobilization efforts including, but not limited to education of stakeholders, engaging diverse populations of multi -ethnic and cultural backgrounds including LGBTQIA communities and organizations, community leaders and residents. Ebony believes those experiences have equipped her to lend her expertise of a well-rounded God -fearing, loving, and faith-filled woman to the world one smile at a time! A graduate of Union University with a degree in Social Science and Biology, she is the single parent of one son, Kahir. Connect with Ebony Wilson via email: ShesThePoisedOne@gmail.com

Britany A. Brooks is a daughter, sister, aunt, friend, and aspiring author who loves the Lord dearly. She is the founder of Godly Women Circle; where women unite and strengthen each other in Christ. She's lives in Kingston, Jamaica where she works in a lead administrative role, at one of the country's most reputable companies. Britany is very enthusiastic about encouraging others to heal from a broken past; and this fuels her desire to further her studies in Psychology. She urges individuals to standardize the following: If hurt people can hurt people then healed people can influence others to heal.

Anita Faye Wilson has always been known for two areas of passion in her life - Ministry and Music. She spent most of her young years sharing the stage with many of the music industry greats including Gloria Estefan. Later she started working behind the scenes as a vocal coach, artist developer and music industry consulting. Wilson was called into the ministry in 1995. Wilson the Evangelist, Coach, Author and Speaker was a 2019 honoree for the United Nations Association of Broward County where she was awarded the Cultural Educator Award. She is Founder of Movement Worldwide Inc. and Eat Well Live Well Be Well LLC.

Bishop Michael Brennen serves as Presiding Bishop of United Christian Wesleyan Methodist Diocese of South Florida, and Pastor of Ebenezer Wesleyan Methodist Church, Delray Beach. He is retired after being employed 30 years by the City of Boca Raton as a Water Treatment Chemist. He is married to Barbara Brennen and together they have a blended family of six children and grandchildren.

Evangelist Teraleen Campbell is an award-winning author, speaker, and certified coach, and serves and intercedes on behalf of the needs of God's people. A survivor of childhood domestic abuse, at the hands of her stepfather, Teraleen is a tireless advocate against domestic violence. Her community involvement has garnered recognition from professional, faith-based, and nonprofit organizations; and her community and ministry extend to Zeta Phi Beta Sorority, Inc. No stranger to providing encouragement through the written word, Teraleen has co-authored five books. Additionally, she released to the award-winning *From Carefree to Caregiver* in 2018. She created Caregivers Connect online support group and through this online community she provides caregivers with resources, support, and training. Her 2021 release *Embracing Your New Normal Devotional* provides support after the loss of a loved one. Connect at Teraleencampbell.com; Facebook, Twitter & Instagram - Teraleen Campbell

Evangelist Mozelle S. Mason is an Associate Pastor at New Birth Baptist Church in Miami, FL., where she served as Pastor of Evangelism and Missions for 7 years. Evangelist Mason returned to the marketplace where she is an Assistant Administrator, for Miami Dade County Public Housing Division.

Having a mantle and a passion for prayer, she currently Hosts monthly THE PRAYER EXPERIENCE dial in prayer call and Praying Through the Pandemic on the Clubhouse app every first and third Saturday.

Evangelist Annette L. Anderson is a Motivational Speaker, Author and Quote-ologist who is passionate about how storytelling, poems, and inspirational messages. She is the author of two books: *Walking It Out* and *Living Life One Quote at A Time*. She believes that if you change your mind set it will be able change your life. She is the founder of "Annette L. Anderson Ministries," a ministry devoted to preaching and teaching the Word of God. She believes that it's important that we all learn to SOAR - Speak! Orate! Articulate! Reverberate!

Metris Batts-Coley is Principal Consultant of The Affiliates, LLC where she coordinates training and workshops for grant writing and volunteer management and consults in the development of nonprofit and for-profit businesses. In her capacity she also serves as a community organizer coordinating cooperative efforts and campaigning to promote the interests of her clients. A woman of faith, she takes joy in posting morning prayers encouraging social media followers.

E Claudette Freeman is an award-winning playwright, novelist, award-winning radio journalist and Publisher and Lead Editor of Pecan Tree Publishing and its imprints. Freeman is the author of three books, two series of journals, a dozen plays and is a sought-after commissioned playwright. When not writing, she loves watching old TV shows, Dateline, and 48 Hours, and sitting in South Florida parks watching iguanas and squirrels do their things. She is the proud mother of one son, Isaiah, and a doggy-grandma to Dolce.

www.ingramcontent.com/pod-product-compliance
Lightning Source LLC
Chambersburg PA
CBHW071058090426
42737CB00013B/2378